篮球英语
BASKETBALL ENGLISH

Author and Illustrator:

Wayon C Collins

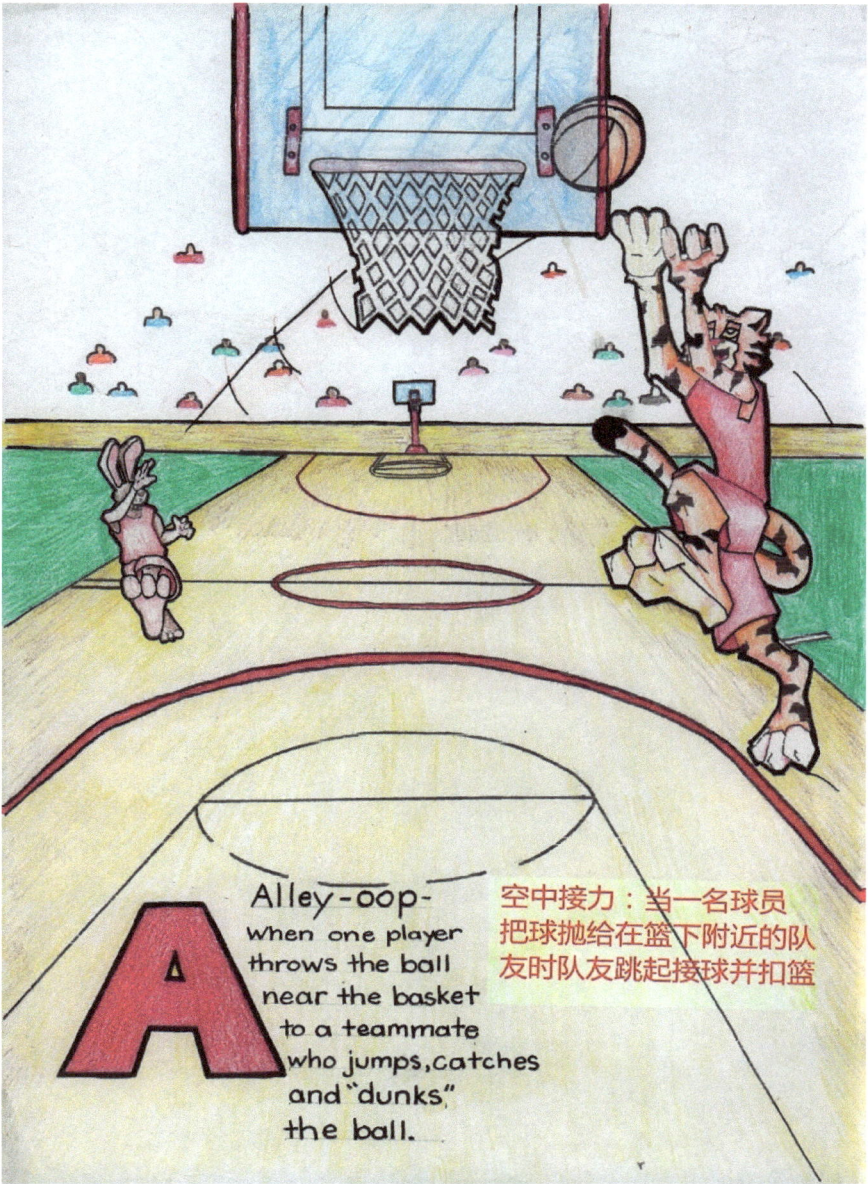

A

Alley-oop- when one player throws the ball near the basket to a teammate who jumps, catches and "dunks" the ball.

空中接力：当一名球员把球抛给在篮下附近的队友时队友跳起接球并扣篮

What words can you think of that start with the letter "A"?

B

班尼　一只拿着篮球的公牛

Benny the bull
is holding a
basketball.

Use a T-chart and have students write tell you words that start
with "A" and "B".

C

Catch: When the ball is secured with both hands after being thrown by another player

接球：当球被另一名球员抛出后用双手接住

When catching a basketball, players fingers should be spread wide as to not hurt their fingers!

扣篮：直接用
单手或者双手
将篮球放进篮
筐得分

Dunk:
To score by
putting the ball
directly through
the basket with
one or both
hands.

Dunking is also called "slam dunk". Dunk entered popular usage in American English, meaning a "sure thing"

D

Dribbling: Bouncing the ball with one hand while walking, running or standing in one spot.

运球：当你在行走，奔跑或者在场上站立时用一只手拍球

Always keep your head up when dribbling at all times. How many foods start with the letter "D"?

E

Elbow: An attempted or actual elbow strike. Violent hits are typically called flagrant fouls.

肘击：企图或实际用肘暴力袭击，通常被称为恶意犯规

What words do you know that start with the letter "E"?

In the 1979–80 season, the NBA adopted the three-point line .

G

Granny shot: This is an underhanded method of shooting a basketball.

The term "Granny shot" is often used as an insult.

奶奶式投篮：这是一种低级的投篮方式 奶奶式投篮作为一个术语经常被用来作为一种侮辱

Allow students to make a T chart. How many words can they think of for "F" and "G"? Talk about these words.

Handles: When a player controls the ball very well.

控球高手：
当一个球员能够很好的控球时的称呼

Seven Things Great Dribblers Do

1. Dribble the ball hard. ...
2. Head up at all times. ...
3. Use your finger tips to control the ball, not your palm.
4. Use your imagination. ...
5. Teach mentality. ...
6. Basketball is a game of length. ...
7. Basketball is also a game of angles. ...

In and out: when the ball enters one side of the rim travels around the rim and exits the opposite side.

一来一往：
篮球由篮筐一侧进入并沿着篮筐转了一圈从另一侧飞出篮筐

To avoid "IN AND OUT", try to shot the ball like a rainbow.

What sweet food starts with the letter "I"?

The letter "I" is called a vowel.

What are the vowels?

J

Jump Ball:
A ball put in play by the referee, who throws it up between two opposing players.

跳球：
由裁判在双方球员中间抛出的球

A jump ball is a method used to begin or resume play in basketball.

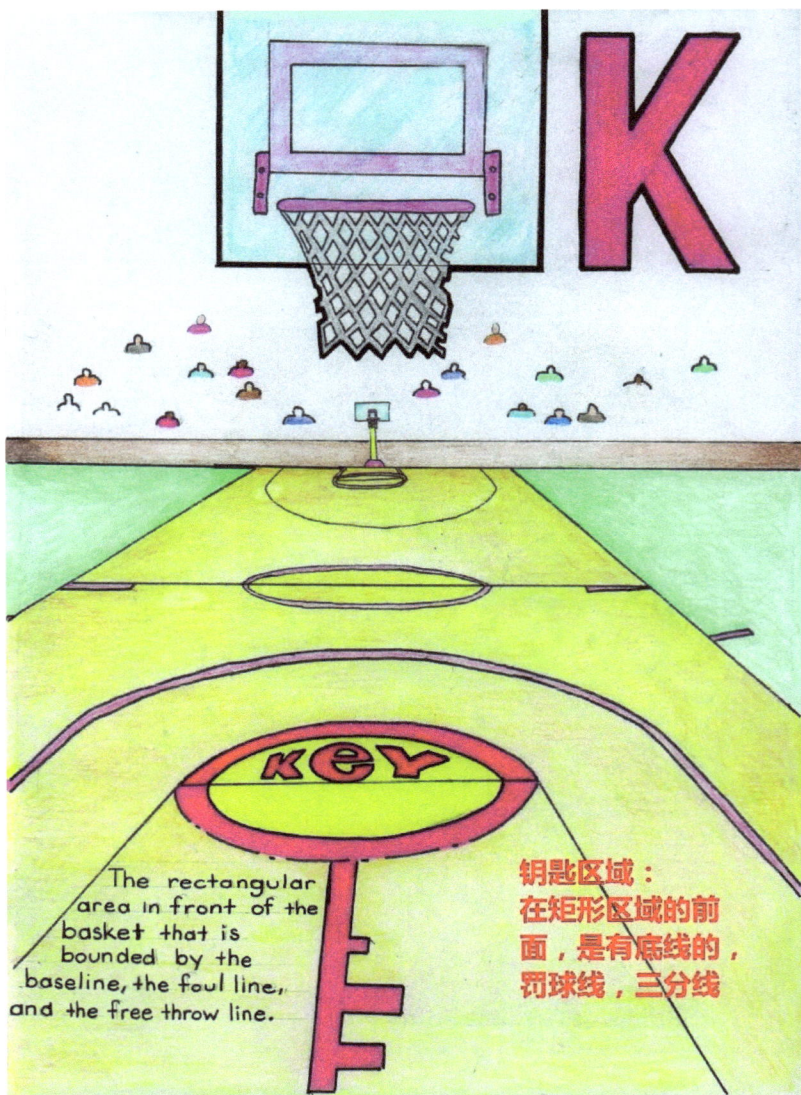

K

KEY

The rectangular area in front of the basket that is bounded by the baseline, the foul line, and the free throw line.

钥匙区域：
在矩形区域的前面，是有底线的，罚球线，三分线

This area of the court is very important in basketball. Whoever controls this area usually gets the most rebounds.

Layup: a two point
shot made by
laying the ball
up near the basket.

上篮：
在篮筐附近将球
打进的二分球

How many words do you know that start with the letter "L"?

M

人盯人：
每一个防守球员被分配
防守一个进攻球员的防守战术

Man to Man is just one of many strategies used in the NBA.
Man to Man is usually used when your team is in much better
physical condition then the other team.

Man to Man is the opposite of Zone Defense.

Teacher should also explain "L" and "M" words using a T chart.

N

No look pass: When offensive player looks in one direction as a fake then throws a pass in another direction without looking at his target.

不看传球：
进攻球员看想一个方向，并没有传球过去，而是在另一个方向抛出一个传球，而不看他的传球目标

How many foods start with the letter "N"?

What kind of shoes start with the letter "N"?

O

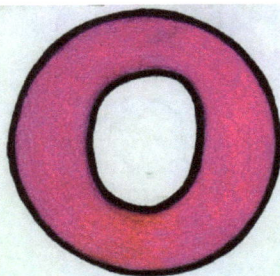

Open palm catch:
The thumbs should touch
hold hands in front of the body.

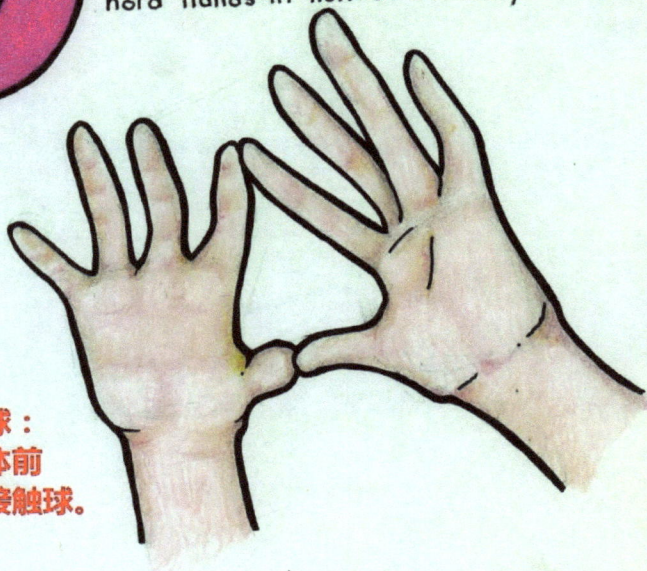

打开手掌接球：
将手举到身体前
方，用手指接触球。

WARNING: It is important to remember to spread your fingers when catching the basketball or else you might suffer a broken finger.

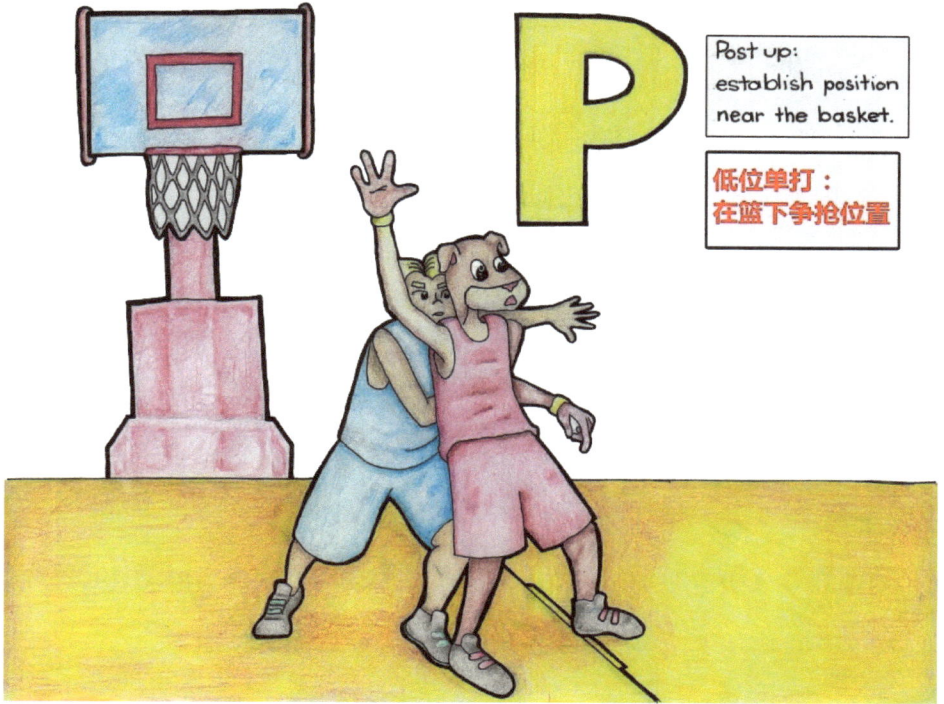

Post up: establish position near the basket.

低位单打：
在篮下争抢位置

Basketball is a physical and mental game. Use both.

A good post defender will bump you so that you lose your balance. Stay low, use fakes and draw fouls when necessary.

Even though size is an advantage, speed and power are more important. Practice your quickness to make the most of your post play.

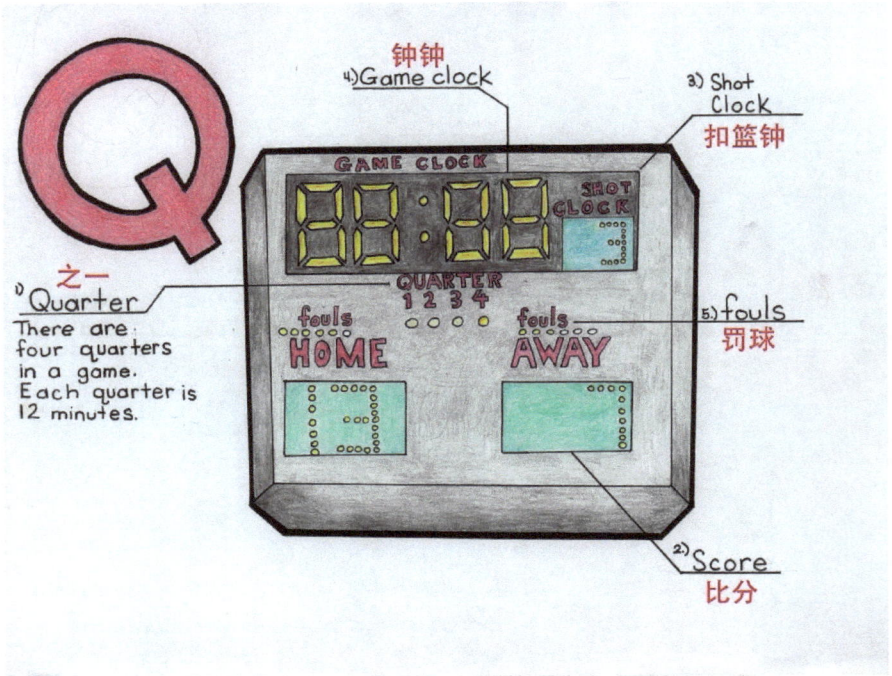

The most important ability in basketball is being <u>QUICK.</u>

In what other <u>sports</u> is being <u>QUICK</u> important?

1. Tennis

2. Baseball

3. Ping Pong

4. Hockey

5. Soccer

6. Boxing

7. Fencing

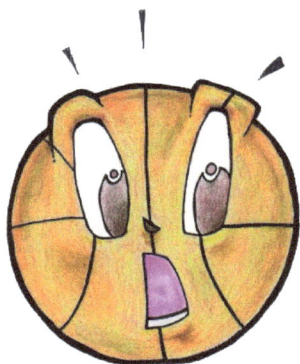

Rock: The slang term for basketball.

石头：篮球俚语

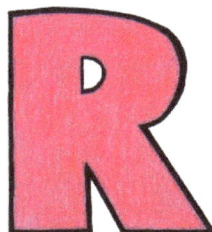

Players usually say "pass me the rock!".

Students should look around the classroom. What things do you see that start with the letter "R"?

"R" is a consonant.

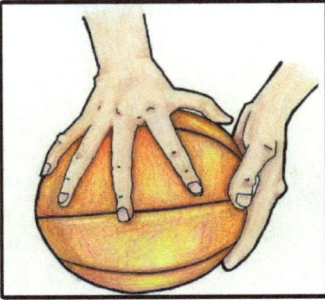

Shooting: Throwing the basketball near the hoop.

投篮：
将篮球抛向篮筐

"Shooting" is one of the most important skills in basketball.

Who are the best shooters in NBA basketball history?

1. Ray Allen, 2,272 shooting points
2. Reggie Miller, 2,226 shooting points
3. Dirk Nowitzki, 1,700 shooting points
4. Steve Nash, 1,677 shooting points
5. Chauncey Billups, 1,537 shooting points

Turnover: When a team loses possession of the ball.

失球：一方球队失去了原来控制着的篮球

All teams want to avoid turnovers. Keeping the safe is very important.

What words do you know that start with the letter "T"?

How many T words can you say in 20seconds?

Uniform:
The same design
worn by all players
on the same team.

U

统一：同一队的
所有球员所穿的
队服是相同的样式

Which team wears your favorite UNIFORM?

ALL students should spell the word UNIFORM.

Player Control
foul
"charging"
球员控制犯规次数

Traveling
走步

Technical foul
技术犯规

Violation: The most minor class of illegal action.

犯规：
最轻微的违法行为

Violations make coaches very angry. Your team can not win with many volations.

Wha words do you know that start with the letter "V"?

After students tell the teacher "V" words have the students play a game of H.O.R.S.E.

W

Walking: When a player moves without dribbling the ball. (traveling)

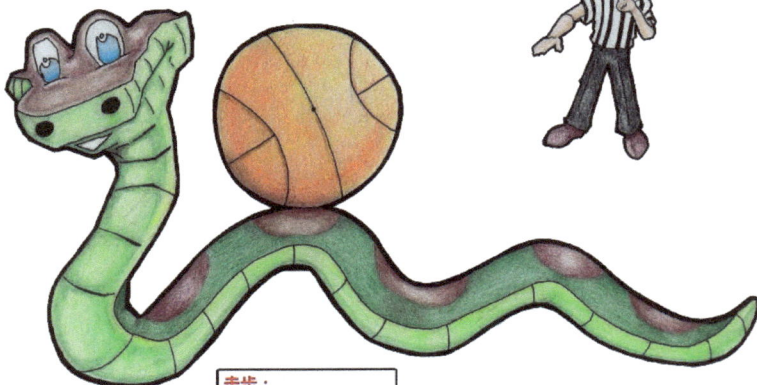

走步：
球员在移动时没有运球

Oh no! Snake has no arms! How can he dribble?

WALKING is a violation.

Xiaochuan Zhai

翟晓川

Xiaochuan plays for the Beijing Ducks. He is a power forward.

Power Forwards are tall and strong.

Who is your favorite player?

How many positions does basketball have?

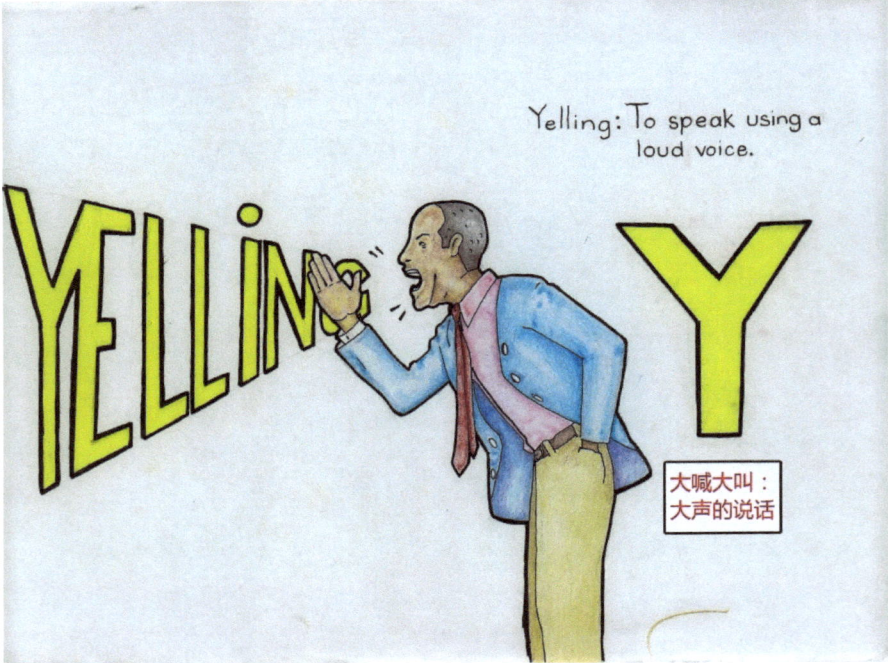

Yelling: To speak using a loud voice.

大喊大叫：大声的说话

What color starts with the letter "Y"?

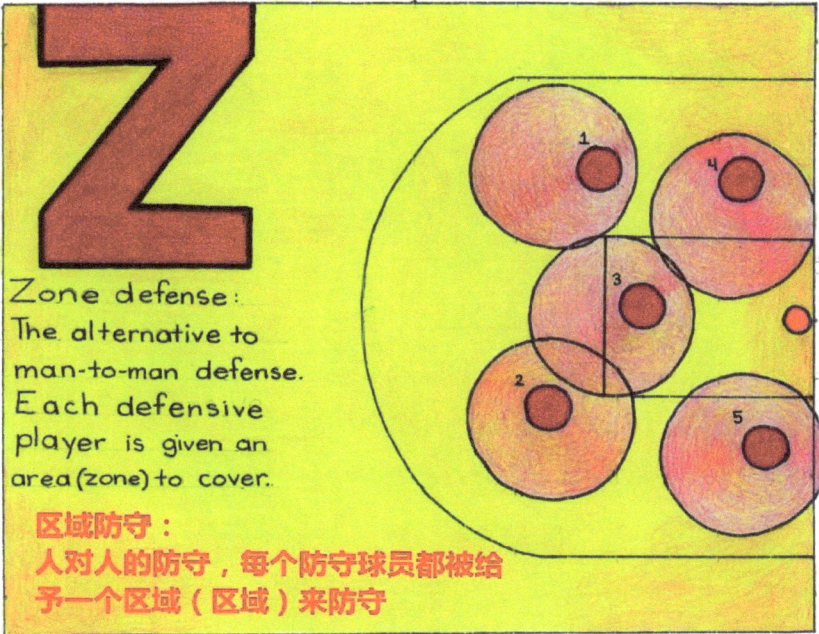

Z

Zone defense:
The alternative to
man-to-man defense.
Each defensive
player is given an
area (zone) to cover.

区域防守：
人对人的防守，每个防守球员都被给
予一个区域（区域）来防守

Zone defense is the opposite of Man of Man.

Tracing Guide

a b c d

e f g h i

j k l m n

o p q r

s t u v w

x y z

Practice writing.

www.ingramcontent.com/pod-product-compliance
Lightning Source LLC
Chambersburg PA
CBHW041805040426
42448CB00001B/42